Monster Trucks

on the Move

Kristin L. Nelson

Lerner Publications Company
Minneapolis

Lerner Publications Company
A division of Lerner Publishing Group, Inc.
241 First Avenue North
Minneapolis, MN 55401 U.S.A.

Website address: www.lernerbooks.com

Library of Congress Cataloging-in-Publication Data

Nelson, Kristin L.
    Monster Trucks on the Move / by Kristin L. Nelson.
        p.   cm. — (Lightning Bolt Books ™ — Vroom-Vroom)
    Includes index.
    ISBN 978-0-7613-6022-3 (lib. bdg. : alk. paper)
    1. Monster trucks—Juvenile literature. I. Title.
 TL230.15.N45 2011
 796.7—dc22   2009038530

Manufactured in the United States of America
2 — BP — 12/1/11

Contents

Giant Machines

What makes this truck different from other trucks?

This truck is a monster truck.
Monster trucks fly through the
air at monster truck shows.
They crush cars.

A monster truck takes off into the air.

Monster trucks race through the mud.

This monster truck sends mud and grass flying.

Swamp Thing looks ready to take a big bite!

They look big and mean—like monsters!

Monster trucks have giant tires. This truck's tires are so big that you could stand up inside them.

Check out these huge tires!

Monster truck tires have thick tread. Tread helps the tires grip the dirt track, so the truck does not slip.

The tread on these tires helps Bigfoot drive through slippery mud.

A monster truck's giant tires are attached to its frame. The frame holds the tires and the body together.

Black Stallion has a blue and green frame and a colorful body.

The driver of this monster truck waves to the crowd as she climbs into the cab.

The driver rides high up in the body. She sits in the cab.

Some monster trucks have special bodies.

This tough truck has muscles!

Look at this truck. It is called Snake Bite. Look at its body. **How do you think Snake Bite got its name?**

Look out for Snake Bite!

Power Trucks

VROOM, VROOM, VROOM!
Monster trucks are louder than other trucks.

A monster truck has a very noisy engine. An engine gives a monster truck power and speed.

A monster truck engine

Monster trucks show off their power at monster truck shows.

People get a chance to see the monster trucks up close at a monster truck show.

Truck Tricks

CRUNCH!

This truck crushes cars with its four big tires.

This monster truck smashes a group of cars.

This truck glides high through the air.

A monster truck leaps over a row of cars at a monster truck show.

This truck stands on its two back wheels. **It is doing a wheelie.**

This truck races in a mud-bogging contest. In a mud-bogging contest, two monster trucks race through thick mud. The winner is the truck that goes farthest through the mud.

Krusher races through the mud.

These two monster trucks race around a track.

The trucks go up a steep ramp during a race. Then they fly over a row of cars. **Where do they land?**

Virginia Giant races up a ramp. It will fly into the air.

This truck lands on a ramp
that slants toward the ground.
Most monster trucks land
safely on all four tires.

Safety First

OUCH! This monster truck has rolled over. Is the driver safe?

A monster truck flips over in this crash.

Yes! Strong metal bars called a roll cage keep the driver from being crushed. The roll cage fits around the top of the cab.

A rescue crew races to help the driver out of his monster truck.

Drivers wear seat belts and helmets for safety too. When do you wear a seat belt or a helmet?

A monster truck driver wears a helmet and a seat belt to stay safe.

Look! This monster truck driver has finished his race safely. He is a winner!

Monster Truck Diagram

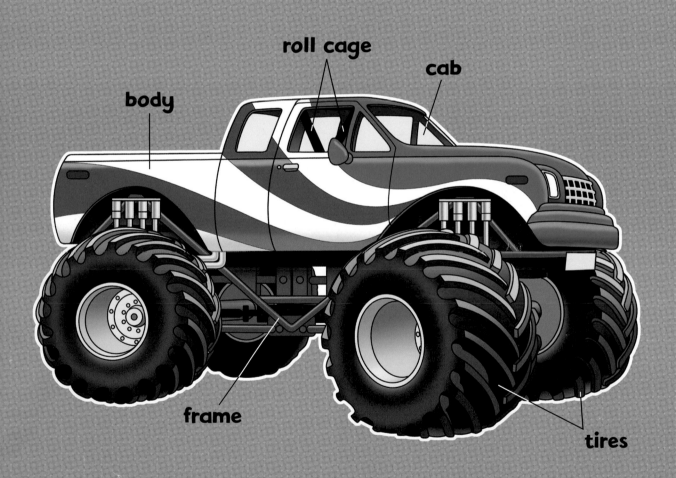

body

roll cage

cab

frame

tires

Fun Facts

- There are two monster trucks that have extra huge tires. Their tires are 10 feet (3 meters) tall. That is as tall as a basketball hoop!

- What would happen if a monster truck drove into a lake? Its giant tires have so much air inside them that the truck would float!

- Some monster trucks have see-through floors. The drivers can see the tires and the track underneath them.

- Most monster trucks do not have real headlights. Headlights are just painted on a monster truck's body. Real headlights are too heavy. They would slow down the truck.

Glossary

body: the main part of a monster truck

engine: the part of a monster truck that gives it the power to move

frame: the part of a monster truck that holds together its main parts, such as the body, tires, and engine

mud-bogging: an event where two monster trucks race through thick mud

roll cage: bars that keep a monster truck driver safe if the truck rolls over

tread: the raised parts of a tire that help it grip the ground and keep it from slipping

wheelie: a monster truck move. A monster truck stands on its two back wheels to do a wheelie.

Further Reading

Brecke, Nicole, and Patricia M. Stockland. *Cars, Trucks, and Motorcycles You Can Draw.* Minneapolis: Millbrook Press, 2010.

Collision Kids
http://www.collisionkids.org

Lyon, George Ella. *Trucks Roll!* New York: Atheneum Books for Young Readers, 2007.

Manolis, Kay. *Monster Trucks.* Minneapolis: Bellwether Media, 2008.

Monster Truck Picture Jigsaw Puzzle
http://www.fun-with-pictures.com/monster-truck-picture-puzzle1.html

Zuehlke, Jeffrey. *Pickup Trucks on the Move.* Minneapolis: Lerner Publications Company, 2011.

Index

Photo Acknowledgments

The images in this book are used with the permission of: Action Images/David and Beverly Huntoon, pp. 1, 2, 4, 5, 6, 8, 9, 10, 11, 12, 13, 14, 15, 16, 17, 19, 21, 22, 23, 24, 25, 26, 27, 30; © Glyn Thomas Photography/Alamy, pp. 7, 29; © Michael Doolittle/Alamy, p. 18; © Satterwhite/TRANSTOCK, p. 20; © Laura Westlund/Independent Picture Service, p. 28; © Tony Watson/Alamy, p. 31.

Front cover: Action Images/David and Beverly Huntoon (both).